DINOSAURS

PARASAUROLOPHUS

BY ANGELA LIM

Kids Core
An Imprint of Abdo Publishing
abdobooks.com

abdobooks.com

Published by Abdo Publishing, a division of ABDO, PO Box 398166, Minneapolis, Minnesota 55439.

Printed in the United States of America, North Mankato, Minnesota.
052025
092025

Cover Photo: Daniel Eskridge/Shutterstock Images
Interior Photos: James Kuether/Science Source, 4–5; iStockphoto, 6, 8, 12–13; Red Line Editorial, 9 (timeline); Shutterstock Images, 9 (dinosaur), 20–21, 25; Danny Ye/Shutterstock Images, 11, 22; Phil Wilson/Stocktrek Images/Science Source, 15; Jose Antonio Penas/Stocktrek Images/Science Source, 16; Daniel Eskridge/Shutterstock Images, 18; Universal Pictures/Photofest, 26; Daniel Eskridge/iStockphoto, 28–29

Editor: Kari Cornell
Series Design: Mary Shaw

Library of Congress Control Number: 2024949830

Publisher's Cataloging-in-Publication Data

Names: Lim, Angela, author.
Title: Parasaurolophus / by Angela Lim
Description: Minneapolis, Minnesota: Abdo Publishing, 2026 | Series: Dinosaurs | Includes online resources and index.
Identifiers: ISBN 9781098297350 (lib. bdg.) | ISBN 9798384919872 (ebook)
Subjects: LCSH: Parasaurolophus--Juvenile literature. | Dinosaurs--Juvenile literature. | Herbivores--Juvenile literature. | Paleontology--Juvenile literature. | Extinct animals--Juvenile literature.
Classification: DDC 568.19--dc23

CONTENTS

Parasaurolophus traveled in herds, moving quickly to confuse predators.

TALKATIVE DINOSAURS

A group of *Parasaurolophus* (peh-ruh-sohr-AH-luh-fuhs) roams through the forest. The dinosaurs make their way through the trees on all fours. As they move, the young *Parasaurolophus* play. They dart between the adults.

Parasaurolophus had more than 1,000 tiny teeth, which it used to grind up plant matter.

Each *Parasaurolophus* has a large crest on top of its head. The heads of the adult dinosaurs rise high into the trees. One dinosaur sniffs the air with its snout. Its pointed snout is shaped like a duck's beak.

The herd stops to rest. The dinosaurs feed on tree leaves. Some *Parasaurolophus* rise up onto their hind legs. They stretch to reach leaves in high branches.

A young *Parasaurolophus* becomes separated from the rest of the herd. It lets out a trumpetlike call with its crest. The sound carries through the forest. An older *Parasaurolophus* hears its cry. It uses its crest to call out. The two continue calling to each other. Finally, the young *Parasaurolophus* returns. It lets out a happy call as it runs alongside its herd.

About Dinosaurs

Parasaurolophus was a dinosaur. There are more than 700 known **species** of dinosaurs.

Parasaurolophus lived at the same time as many other dinosaurs, including *Tyrannosaurus rex*.

Dinosaurs were reptiles that lived during the Mesozoic Era. This time period lasted from 252 to 66 million years ago. *Parasaurolophus* lived from about 77 to 73 million years ago.

When *Parasaurolophus* Lived

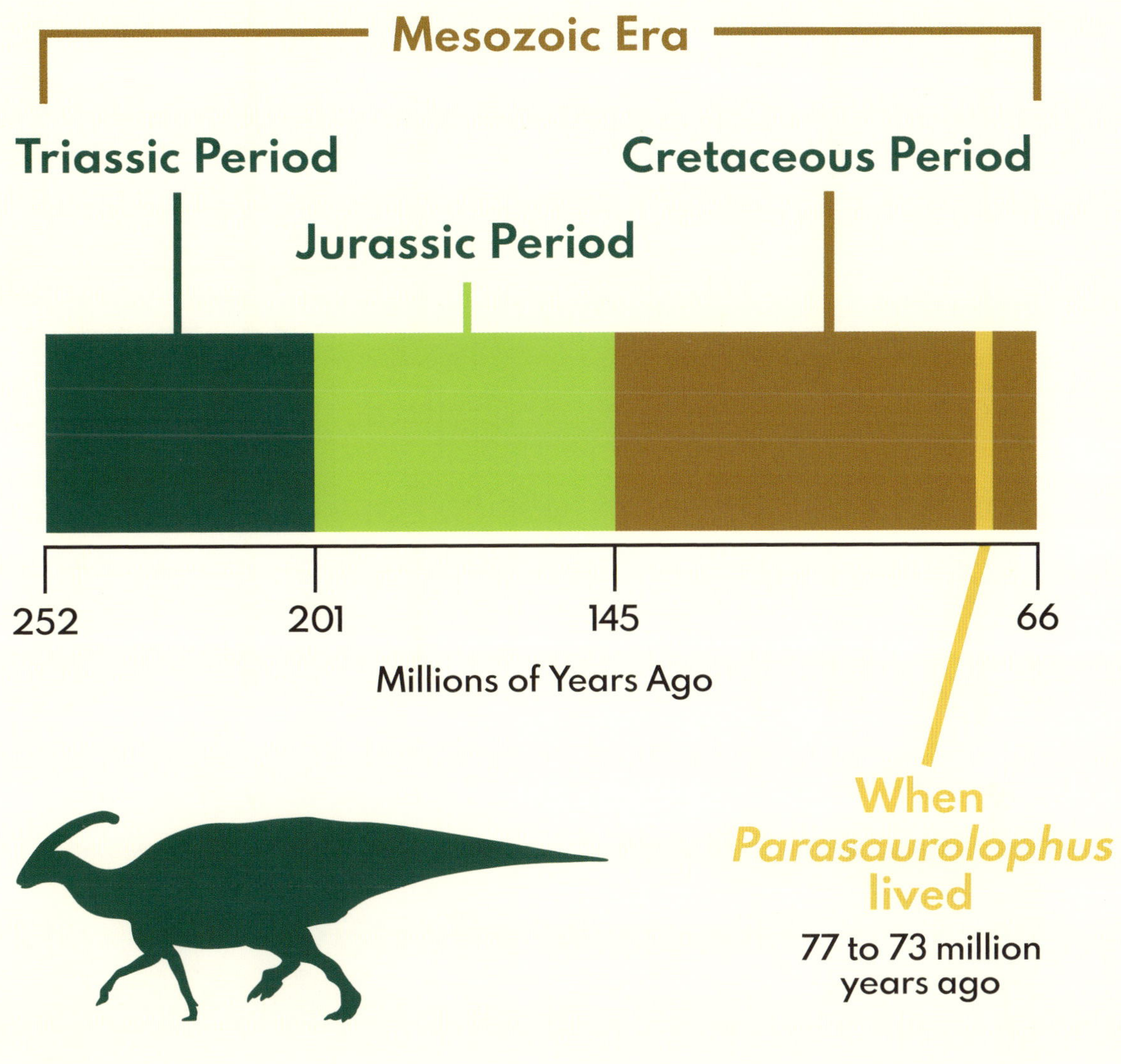

The Mesozoic Era lasted for millions of years. It can be divided into three periods. *Parasaurolophus* lived at the end of the Cretaceous period.

Dinosaurs went **extinct** at the end of the Mesozoic Era. At that time, a huge asteroid from space crashed into Earth. It caused extreme weather. It also caused a huge shift in **climate**. Dinosaurs were not able to survive.

Today, **paleontologists** learn about dinosaurs by studying fossils. Fossils are the remains of animals and plants. These remains were buried underground for thousands

Dinosaurs Today

Some flying dinosaurs survived the asteroid strike. Over millions of years, these dinosaurs **evolved** into birds. Today, birds are the only living animals related to dinosaurs.

A cast model of a *Parasaurolophus* skull shows the hollow tubes of the dinosaur's crest.

of years. They became rock. Paleontologists study *Parasaurolophus* fossils to learn what the dinosaur looked like and how it behaved.

Explore Online

Visit the website below. Does it give any new information about dinosaurs that wasn't in Chapter One?

Dinosaur

abdocorelibrary.com/parasaurolophus

Parasaurolophus ate vegetation of all kinds, including ferns, pine twigs, and tree bark.

CHAPTER 2

PARASAUROLOPHUS APPEARANCE

Dinosaur bones can become fossils. *Parasaurolophus* bones show that it was a large dinosaur. It was 29.5 feet (9 m) long. This is about half the length of a bowling lane. *Parasaurolophus* was also a heavy dinosaur.

It weighed about 3.3 tons (3 metric tons). This is about how much an African elephant weighs.

Its large size protected *Parasaurolophus* against predators. Small predators were unable to hunt *Parasaurolophus* on their own. The dinosaur also traveled in herds. This made it difficult for predators to attack one dinosaur within the group.

Fossils of *Parasaurolophus* teeth have also been found. The dinosaur's jaw held hundreds of teeth. But only a few teeth were used at a time. The teeth would become worn down from eating tough plant material.

Imprints of body parts can also become fossils. These are called trace fossils. Skin can become a trace fossil. The texture of a dinosaur's

Tiny teeth packed *Parasaurolophus*'s duck-like bill. When teeth wore out, the dinosaur simply used others to chew sticks and sturdy leaves and grasses.

skin is pressed into mud. New **sediment** fills the imprint. It hardens into rock. The rock takes on the texture of the imprint. Trace fossils show that *Parasaurolophus* had scales.

Scientists noticed that *Parasaurolophus*'s scales were different sizes and shapes. These different types of scales formed a striped pattern.

Paleontologists have discovered *Parasaurolophus* skulls. The skulls show that the dinosaur was a hadrosaur. This means it had a duck-like bill. *Parasaurolophus* skulls also have a hollow crest.

The crest of *Parasaurolophus* may have influenced mating. Females may have chosen a mate with a larger crest.

The crest also helped produce sound. *Parasaurolophus* were able to communicate with one another. It is likely that the dinosaurs could recognize one another by voice. *Parasaurolophus* also may have made warning sounds when predators were near.

Creating the Sound of *Parasaurolophus*

Scientists took **CT scans** of *Parasaurolophus* skulls and crests. Then computer scientists designed a program. It recreated the sound of the dinosaur based on its crest shape. The program showed that *Parasaurolophus* made a low rumbling sound. The dinosaur could also change the pitch of its voice.

The sound *Parasaurolophus* made with its crest has been compared to the sound of an elephant trumpeting.

Parasaurolophus Behavior

Parasaurolophus ate plants. It mainly ate pine needles and other leaves from trees. The dinosaur walked around on four legs. But it may have been able to stand on its hind legs. This would help it reach leaves. Experts are still studying *Parasaurolophus* to determine whether it could walk on two legs.

PRIMARY SOURCE

Carl Diegert worked to digitally create the call of *Parasaurolophus*. He described the sound:

> The sound may have been somewhat birdlike, and it's probably not unreasonable to think they did songs of some sort to call one another.

Source: Chris Miller. "Digital Paleontology: Producing the Sound of the *Parasaurolophus* Dinosaur." *Sandia National Laboratories*, 19 Dec. 1997, sandia.gov. Accessed 30 Sept. 2024.

Comparing Texts

Think about the quote. Does it support the information in this chapter? Or does it give a different perspective? Explain how in a few sentences.

The *Parasaurolophus* skeleton at the Field Museum in Chicago, Illinois, is a holotype. That means this skeleton is used as a guide to see if another dinosaur is from the same species.

CHAPTER 3

DISCOVERING PARASAUROLOPHUS

The Royal Ontario Museum sent a team of scientists to Alberta, Canada, in 1920. The scientists were looking for dinosaur fossils. They found a dinosaur skull and other bones. William A. Parks was on one of the teams of scientists that found the dinosaur fossils.

Parasaurolophus walkeri was one of three species of the dinosaur.

He wrote about the discovery. He also named the dinosaur *Parasaurolophus*.

Parasaurolophus was not the first duck-billed dinosaur to be discovered in Canada. Paleontologist Barnum Brown had discovered another hadrosaur in Alberta in 1911. He called that dinosaur *Saurolophus* in 1912.

Saurolophus means "lizard crest." Parks thought the new dinosaur looked like *Saurolophus*. He chose the name *Parasaurolophus*, which means "like *Saurolophus*."

Both dinosaurs had a crest. But *Parasaurolophus* had a longer crest. The structure of the *Parasaurolophus* crest puzzled paleontologists.

They came up with many possible uses for the crest. One idea was that the dinosaur used its crest like a snorkel. It would help dinosaurs breathe while eating underwater plants. But there was no opening on the crest. Some thought the crest helped *Parasaurolophus* smell. Others thought it helped the dinosaur control its body temperature.

Paleontologists came up with a new **theory** in 1981. They thought the crest had two main uses. It was used as a visual display. It also helped the dinosaurs communicate. This is the most well-supported theory to date.

People can see *Parasaurolophus* skeletons on display at the Field Museum in Chicago, Illinois. They can also visit the Alf Museum of Paleontology in California. A baby *Parasaurolophus* skull is displayed there.

Dinosaur Provincial Park

The site where *Parasaurolophus* was discovered is now a part of Dinosaur Provincial Park. The area was first protected in 1955. More than 35 dinosaur species have been discovered in the park.

Dinosaur bones were first discovered in the Red Deer River valley in Alberta, Canada, by Joseph B. Tyrrell in 1884. The site is now home to Dinosaur Provincial Park.

Parasaurolophus in Media

Parasaurolophus is a popular dinosaur in films. A herd of *Parasaurolophus* was shown in the movie *Jurassic World Dominion* (2022).

Owen Grady, played by Chris Pratt, rides alongside a pair of *Parasaurolophus* in *Jurassic World Dominion.*

The dinosaurs ran on two legs in the movie. However, paleontologists do not know how often these dinosaurs moved on two legs.

Several *Parasaurolophus* are shown eating in Pixar's *The Good Dinosaur*. They appear to stand on two legs as they eat plants from the ground. But fossils of *Parasaurolophus* teeth suggest the dinosaur ate tree leaves.

Depictions of *Parasaurolophus* in media may not be accurate. But scientists have learned a lot about these dinosaurs. They know how *Parasaurolophus* used its crest to communicate. They even know how the dinosaur may have sounded. They continue to learn more about *Parasaurolophus*.

Further Evidence

Look at the website below. Does it give any new evidence to support Chapter Three?

How Are Dinosaur Fossils Formed?

abdocorelibrary.com/parasaurolophus

DINO DETAILS

Scaly skin like reptiles today

Primarily walked on four legs to support its weight

Hollow crest used for communicating and attracting mates
Duck-like bill filled with teeth for chewing plants

Glossary

climate
average weather conditions in an area over a long period of time

CT scans
three-dimensional X-ray images of a part inside the body

evolved
changed over time

extinct
no longer exists

paleontologist
a scientist who studies fossils

sediment
soil that is moved around by water, wind, or ice

species
a group of similar living things that can produce young with one another

theory
an idea that is based on fact or knowledge

Online Resources

To learn more about *Parasaurolophus* and late-Cretaceous dinosaurs, visit our free resource websites below.

Visit **abdocorelibrary.com** or scan this QR code for free Common Core resources for teachers and students, including vetted activities, multimedia, and booklinks, for deeper subject comprehension.

Visit **abdobooklinks.com** or scan this QR code for free additional online weblinks for further learning. These links are routinely monitored and updated to provide the most current information available.

Learn More

Dinosaur Atlas. National Geographic, 2022.

Kuether, James. *Dinosaurs for Kids.* Adventure, 2024.

Murray, Julie. *Parasaurolophus.* Abdo, 2025.

Index

About the Author

Angela Lim is an MFA student in poetry at Indiana University. *Stegosaurus* is her favorite dinosaur.